Analyze Your Personality Through Color

by Alfred W. Munzert, Ph.D.

Monarch Press NEW YORK

Published by MONARCH PRESS
A Simon & Schuster Division of Gulf & Western Corporation
Simon & Schuster Building
1230 Avenue of the Americas
New York, New York 10020

Manufactured in the United States of America
10 9 8 7 6 5 4 3 2 1

ISBN: 0-671-34036-0

Contents

Introduction

This book is your ticket to new adventures in exploring life through the world of color! Color is a very important part of your life. Your favorite colors are reflected in your home and in the colors of the clothing you wear.

It would be difficult to overestimate the dynamic role that color plays in your everyday life. Even your emotional and physical well-being is strongly influenced by the colors around you.

Of far greater significance, but little understood, however, is the fact that color can actually be a key to unlocking the secrets of your personality.

Few people are aware of the amazing accuracy of color in analyzing personality. Only in recent years has scientific study shown that color psychology is a simple and effective clue to personality analysis. In fact, analysis through color may be far more accurate than measurement through more traditional methods. The reasons for this are really quite simple.

A major difficulty in most psychological testing is the fact that many people attempt to hide their true motivations and emotions. Since traditional forms of psychological tests are often quite threatening because they are clouded in the mystique of professional analysis, people have the tendency to try to outguess the test and to give the "right" or "best" answer. Even beyond the fear of revealing themselves to others, most people are only vaguely aware of their inner motivations, feelings, and attitudes and have difficulty articulating them under the best of intentions.

However, color as a testing device is completely disarming and can even be entertaining. People see no threat whatsoever in color and tend to respond freely and spontaneously to it. In so doing, they convey unusually revealing and accurate pictures of their personalities.

You can use the test in this book to discover new and interesting facets of your innermost feelings, goals, and behaviors. In addition, this new knowledge gained of yourself and others through personality analysis can be applied to determine the degree of compatibility between two or more human beings.

The Personality and Compatibility Indexes which follow have been designed to give a simple but accurate analysis of basic personality traits through the use of only eight basic colors. While complete in-depth psychoanalysis requires extensive testing and professional evaluation, you will be amazed at the insight which you will gain through this simplified version of color testing.

In addition to evaluating the personality of yourself and others, the Compatibility Index (keyed to the color chart on the back cover) will further help you to determine the degree of compatibility between two or more personality types. Finding out more about your own personality and your compatibility with the people important to your life can be both useful and entertaining.

The second test, at the end of the book, will help you to determine your color quotient. A series of simulation games will demonstrate how a knowledge of color can help you to evaluate a great variety of human situations. You will also find this an interesting opportunity to apply your new knowledge of color to real-life situations.

Before you test your color quotient and apply your newly gained knowledge of color, you will also have an opportunity to find out more about the history and psychology of color. Since the earliest days of humankind, color has been a significant force in people's lives; color has been used to chase away evil, gain comfort, heal the human body, and much more. With humans, the effects of color are so closely intertwined with self-survival and life-necessities that the impact of color upon the human organism is universal, cutting across both time and culture barriers.

This book is a simplified version of an in-depth and exacting body of knowledge and psychological testing devices. As such, it presents the best probabilities under normal conditions. It does not provide the necessary text, nor is it intended, to provide a manual of training in either psychology or the science of color psychology. Upon completing the tests and games in this book, you will have been exposed to some interesting and entertaining concepts which can be explored in greater depth and exactitude, if you are so inclined.

The color quotient "test" is not a test in the formal sense of the word. Your score on the test will not reveal your knowledge of color as related to the rest of the population, but will give you an indication of your understanding of the simplified principles presented in this book. In terms of color application, there is often no one "right" answer, but several which might be acceptable solutions, depending upon the complexity of a particular situation.

The compatibility test is based upon the most probable results of persons exhibiting the normal outward behaviors of a particular personality type. It is an indicator, a guide, and a framework which is not based upon any absolute set of factors.

When you finish this book, you will not be a color psychologist or a color scientist, but you will be much more knowledgeable about the impact of color on life than you were before. So sit back, relax, and begin a fascinating journey into the simplified secrets of color.

Part I Personality-Compatibility Index

Your Personality Through Color

Sections One, Two, and Three of this test will help you to discover your basic personality traits and the psychological significance of liking or disliking specific colors.

Instructions for Taking the Test

1. Do no further reading beyond this page at this time, except as directed in the instructions.
2. Turn immediately to the back cover and examine the color chart. From the colors shown, select the color that you most prefer. (Your first reaction is the best.)
3. After selecting your preferred color, choose the color that you like second best.
4. Finally, select the color that you like the least. In each instance, your first reaction is the most accurate.
5. After making these three selections, first turn to Section One of the test and locate the paragraph describing the color of your first choice and read it.
6. When you have completed reading the appropriate paragraph from Section One, turn to Section Two of the test, locate the paragraph that refers to the color of your second choice, and read that.
7. After you have completed the readings from Sections One and Two, turn to Section Three, locate the paragraph which describes your least-liked color, and read that.

You will now have a composite description of your basic personality in terms of behaviors, goals, and unsatisfied needs. Read the introduction to each section of the test to clarify the meaning of each selected color and the rejected color. Over a period of time your selections and rejections may change. This is natural and indicates the fact that humans are subject to continuous and ongoing change and growth.

Compatibility Through Color

Have two or more people select their first color choices, then locate these two colors on, first, the Color Compatibility Chart on the back cover and, second, in the appropriate segment of the Compatibility Analysis which begins on page 13.

It is important to understand that the compatibility chart and index are based only upon the first color choice, which indicates behavior. One must also take into account the second color choice, which will have some effect upon the positive or negative aspects of one's basic behavior. In addition, the chart and index are basic guides, not infallible rules. For example, while a blue and a purple personality are basically incompatible, such factors as motivation to establish or continue a relationship will play a part in the real-life success of such a combination. The compatibility analysis provided here will, however, make it possible for two or more people to identify potential sources of basic conflict and work around those to make a relationship more productive and successful. The analysis provided may also be valuable as an aid in understanding past sources of conflict and working in a positive manner to resolve such difficulties in a productive and mature manner.

Keep in mind, also, that color selections will change over a period of time. They are also subject to short-term change, as they may be affected by mood and circumstances as well as maturity, personal growth, and changing goals and needs.

Section One—First Color Preference

Significance of the First Color Choice

From the chart on the back cover, you have selected the two colors that appeal to you most. This selection is highly significant in evaluating your personality.

The *first* color choice—the one that you liked the most—describes your *basic* personality traits. These traits form the image that you project and which other people see. These basic traits are the means or methods of behavior by which you attempt to reach your goals. They describe your basic behavior-style.

From the following section, read carefully the personality profile which corresponds to your color preference. This will describe your basic personality traits.

If Your First Choice Is Red

If you prefer red, you are an aggressive person with strong desires and a craving for action. You are energetic, impulsive, have a tremendous drive for success, and often find yourself in the middle of the action that you crave. You are quick to take sides and to make judgments. However, you are not unreasonably stubborn, and, in fact, may be sometimes too easily swayed in your feelings and attitudes.

You are an extrovert who plunges headlong into the adventure of living and you eagerly search for a variety of experiences. You reject monotony in any form and your search for activity may sometimes make you appear fickle. You tend to lack perseverance, but may reach success through sheer energy and force of personality.

For you, the issues of life are clear-cut and dramatic and you tend toward extremes in all that you do. This also applies to your temper, moods, attitudes, and emotions. Since you believe that happiness is the natural state of affairs, you are involved in an endless pursuit of excitement, for this is your road to happiness. However, you should be careful to avoid the tendency to blame others for your failures, for this could be a decided weakness in what is otherwise an extremely strong personality.

If Your First Choice Is Blue

If you prefer blue, you have a basic need for a calm, harmonious, tension-free existence. This inner demand for tranquility has a vital impact upon your personality. Because you dislike upsets and disturbances, you are inclined to be somewhat cautious in the way you dress, act, and speak. You like to be admired for your calm, steady behavior and are generally a conscientious worker in whatever you do.

While you make a loyal and trustworthy friend, you may tend to be self-centered, egotistical, and sometimes impatient with the ideas of others, especially if they differ from your own. You are skeptical of strangers because they represent unknown and possibly upsetting situations. While you are sociable, you prefer people of similar backgrounds to your own, since they present less of a threat to the harmony so important to your life. You have a great deal of faith in other people and expect them to have similar faith in you.

If you are a blue personality, happiness is not viewed as a natural state; therefore, you are delighted when it does occur. You may, however, be too prone to accept a life that is not brimming with happiness.

If Your First Choice Is Green

A preference for green indicates stability, balance, and persistence. When you start something, you finish it! You are the good citizen, the respectable neighbor, and the concerned parent. You are conscientious about voting, joining clubs, and supporting local organizations. In fact, belonging to the most fashionable or the best clubs is very important to you, for it is there that you will be in contact with the "right" people. You are inclined to be frank, moral, and sensitive to social etiquette. Your reputation is highly important to you, but you do take a certain delight in hearing of the scandals of other people.

You are generally affectionate and a loyal friend, lover, and spouse. While you are probably intelligent and educated, you are likely to do the expected and accepted thing rather than to introduce innovation.

Because of your balance and stability, you are unlikely to have emotional problems, but you are in constant need of having affectionate friends and family, receiving respect from others, and attaining personal success.

If Your First Choice Is Yellow

Yellow indicates a yearning for the new, the modern, and an expanding future. If you prefer yellow, you are inclined to be intellectual, idealistic, and highly imaginative. Yellow is the color of the creative and artistic individual. You may often find yourself involved in cults, reform movements, or innovation. Despite your idealism, you may be rather shy and hesitant with other people. Your convictions are profound and genuine, having been carefully thought out. Because of this depth of feeling, you may tend to be impatient with others, causing you to appear aloof.

You are driven by lofty ideas and are more likely to dwell in theory than to take concrete action. You have a well-controlled temper and are genuinely concerned with the well-being and future of society, although individual persons may antagonize you.

If you are a yellow personality, you should take care to avoid overindulgence in fantasy and should strive to be more liberal toward the viewpoints of other people.

If Your First Choice Is Purple

If you prefer purple, you may believe that you are set apart and unique from other people. This belief may lead you to exhibit aloofness and a concern about yourself and your appearance. You are highly sensitive and observant and may be quite temperamental in your behavior. In fact, although you are generally tolerant, you can be quite sarcastic if you feel the occasion calls for it.

It is very likely that you are highly talented artistically and prefer a world of fantasy to the world of reality. Often your behavior is inconsistent or indecisive. While you may become outraged at the misfortunes of humanity, you will be inclined to do little about them.

You enjoy impressing others with a display of creativity, glamour, or authority. Because of your tolerance, you are an easy person to live with, but will avoid a relationship which includes excessive obligations. You may confide freely in close friends, perhaps to ward off a feeling of loneliness, but it is often difficult for them to completely understand your personality.

If Your First Choice Is Brown

A preference for brown indicates a steady, reliable character. You have a keen sense of duty and rarely shirk responsibility. Your devotion to duty may in fact lead others to take advantage of you, causing you at times to feel persecuted. Since you live by deeply ingrained habits, you may have very strong views and you may tend to be intolerant of others who are impulsive or rash. You have a natural talent and shrewdness for managing money, both your own and that of others.

You have a strong need at all times for physical well-being, security, and a sense of belonging so you place great emphasis upon home and family.

If Your First Choice Is Black

If you prefer black, you are greatly dissatisfied with existing circumstances. You feel pressured by forces beyond your control and you rebel against accepting things as they are. You want to be master of your own destiny and may wish to strike out against the unfair scheme of things which surrounds you.

You carry yourself with dignity and wish to impress others with your worldliness. You are inclined to conceal your real personality and emotions from others. You find it difficult to be carefree, but in public you may put forward an image of wit and cleverness to those around you.

If Your First Choice Is Gray

If you prefer gray, you have a deep desire to conceal yourself from the world. You wish to protect yourself from the pressures of our hectic society. You are reluctant to become involved, and therefore avoid committing yourself completely to anything. Thus, your participation in most things is superficial and detached and often you simply merely go through the motions.

A choice of gray indicates a significant yearning for the ease and quiet that comes with non-involvement. You may already have tired of life's struggles and seek a peaceful existence free from conflict and turmoil.

Section Two— Second Color Preference

Significance of Second Color Choice

While your first color preference shows the means or method of behavior by which you attempt to reach your goals, the second choice points out *what* your goal is. Since this real goal, which may or may not be obvious, plays a significant role in directing your actual behavior, you may have felt that the first personality profile was more or less exaggerated. You should realize, however, that your objective or goal influences the direction and the degree to which these basic traits are developed in your personality. A knowledge of your basic goal combined with your basic personality traits will give you a far greater insight into yourself as an individual. The difference in goals (second color) also explains why two people of the same personality type (first color) may exhibit quite different behavior.

It is only by combining the meanings of the first and second color preferences that a clearer understanding of personality can be arrived at.

From the following paragraphs, locate your second color choice. After examining the description of your goal, carefully weigh this goal against the profile given in Section One. For example, a first color choice of red combined with a second color choice of blue would have decidedly different implications than a first color of red and a second choice of yellow. The first combination would result in a more tempered approach to life and probably be manifest in an individual who is assertive, energetic, and self-motivated toward balanced, dynamic forms of success, while the second combination would more likely be seen as an assertive, energetic, outgoing, open personality whose strength and drive are demonstrated through creative, optimistic, and energetic activity.

When you have examined both the personality and the goal descriptions of your first and second color choices, you will have a more complete understanding of your basic goal and of the methods you use to achieve that goal.

If Your Second Choice Is Red

The selection of red as a second color choice indicates that your basic goal in life is to achieve an exciting, adventurous life-style which is filled with activity and happiness.

If Your Second Choice Is Blue

If blue is chosen as a second color choice, it indicates that your major objective is having a harmonious and tranquil existence which is free from strife.

If Your Second Choice Is Green

The choice of green as a second color selection indicates that your major goal is to gain recognition and acceptance of your views as an individual.

If Your Second Choice Is Yellow

Since yellow is the color of hope and yearning, a selection of yellow as a second choice indicates that your objective is to be involved in things that are new and hold the promise of a better future.

If Your Second Choice Is Purple

The choice of purple as a second color indicates that your major goal is to fascinate and enchant others. In turn, you also seek stimulation from others.

If Your Second Choice Is Brown

Your major drive, indicated by the choice of brown as a second color, is for complete security and physical and mental comfort.

If Your Second Choice Is Black

A selection of black as a second choice indicates that your major drive in life is to avoid being dominated or influenced in your life-style.

If Your Second Choice Is Gray

Your selection of gray as a second color choice signifies that your goal is to be uninvolved in the pressures of life and society.

Section Three— Color Rejection

Significance of Color Rejection

In Sections One and Two, you discovered that your first color preference gave a profile of your basic personality traits and that your second color preference indicated your basic goal or objective.

The rejection or dislike of a color is highly significant because it indicates an unsatisfied basic need in your personality which is causing you stress or anxiety. From the following segments, locate the color you rejected and read the accompanying description to gain still further insight into your personality.

After completing this section, you will be aware of:

1. Your basic goal (from the second color)
2. Your anxiety or problem (from the rejected color)
3. Your method of behavior for reaching your goal and for solving your problem (from the first color)

By combining these three, you will have a very important key to understanding yourself as an individual.

If You Rejected Red

A dislike of red gives evidence that you feel frustrated and defeated. Despite tremendous efforts on your part, you feel that life has not rewarded your struggle. You long for peace and security, but seem unable to find it. You feel threatened by the intensity and aggression surrounding you, but there seems to be no escape. As a result, you have an overwhelming feeling of helplessness.

If You Rejected Blue

A dislike of blue indicates that you feel trapped in an unhappy environment and are unable to change it. You are tired of trying to cope with the situation, and your frustration is causing you to be irritable and possibly even neurotic. You feel a strong desire to escape from the situation, possibly to quit your job or leave home, but you are in conflict because you feel dependent upon them. You long for a more exciting life which you feel has been denied to you.

If You Rejected Green

A dislike of green gives evidence that you feel betrayed by society and that your failure as an individual is due to that betrayal. Your need to impress and to be recognized as an unusual individual has not been fulfilled, and this failure makes you feel hostile to those around you. You are reluctant to become involved and have probably retreated into a lonely and troubled existence.

If You Rejected Yellow

Rejection of yellow indicates that you have become a pessimist. Your hopes and dreams have not been fulfilled and you have suffered deep disappointment. You're going to stick to the practical, down-to-earth things that you know you can accomplish. People who go around with their heads in the clouds are foolish, and you're not going to get caught in that kind of nonsense again.

If You Rejected Purple

A rejection of purple means that you value frankness and sincerity above all other qualities. You dislike those who "put on airs" and pretend to be something they are not. This need for sincerity tends to make you rather reserved and aloof, for you are reluctant to become involved unless you know precisely the nature of the involvement and to where it will lead.

If You Rejected Brown

A dislike of brown indicates a drive for recognition. You want to stand out as an individual. You are probably generous and quick-witted and you can "think on your feet." You reject the humdrum conventional ways and are inclined to be impatient with slower, less capable people than yourself. Others may be undecided, but not you. You know where you are going, and you look forward to the exciting things that life has to offer.

If You Rejected Black

Black represents the absolute—the insolvable mystery of death and eternity. A rejection of black signifies a desire to resist fate and to be master of your own destiny. You resent demands made upon you and are determined to surrender nothing. Those who attempt to restrict or control your actions are going to meet with fierce resistance.

If You Rejected Gray

A dislike of gray indicates a restless boredom with your life. You are tired of the monotonous life you lead and long for excitement. You are not quite certain what kind of excitement you crave, but you are impatient for a richer and fuller existence. This frustration may lead you to jump headlong into one involvement after another in a frantic and sometimes unhappy pursuit of exciting experiences.

Compatibility

The Compatibility Index

In the first part you were given a dramatic illustration of your basic personality through color analysis. Now, the compatibility index will provide an illustration of the further significance of color as an indicator of human compatibility or the lack of such compatibility.

It is important to remember that this is not a hard and fast guide to compatibility. Many factors need consideration which cannot be accommodated in such a simplified version of compatibility testing. A complete and in-depth analysis of compatibility requires more extensive testing and information than that which can be applied through just one color preference. However, based on normal probabilities of basic personality traits and behaviors, it is possible to establish a fairly accurate guide to compatibility on the basis of this one color preference. As stated previously, the second color choice, motivation of individuals to maintain a relationship, and other factors will make the final determination of compatibility in a real-life situation. Along with the index which follows, you may use the chart on the back cover as a quick index of potential agreement or conflict between basic personality types described here.

Red-Red Combination

Two basic red personalities may be highly compatible. Each one's admiration for the other's strength, energy, and drive can be the basis for great mutual attraction. Intellectually, each will be highly sympathetic to the other's frequently impulsive and rash behavior. Because each is highly motivated by a craving for adventure and action, two red individuals will find each other's company highly stimulating.

However, conflict may arise if the two red personalities find themselves competing in the same arena or on the same issue. In such cases, since the basic red personality is given to extremes of mood and behavior, there could well be a fight to the finish. If these two, however, can avoid competition, they will make an impressive and dynamic combination.

Red-Gray Combination

These two personalities are basically incompatible. The gray personality is seeking escape from the pressures of the world and is highly reluctant to become involved in any endeavor whatsoever. This attitude of non-involvement is in direct conflict with the basic red personality, which craves excitement and involvement.

Since the personalities of red and gray are in direct opposition to each other, such a relationship could well be one of frustration and bitter unhappiness.

Red-Green Combination

This combination is basically incompatible. There will be almost constant conflict because of the differences in methods, life-styles, and behaviors.

Whereas the red personality uses impulsive and unorthodox methods, the green personality is methodical and conventional in approaches to life. While the green personality has a deep respect for tradition, social etiquette, and the established system, the red, on the contrary, is inclined to be irreverent and impatient with the existing society. Red is the reformer and the innovator. The green personality is horrified by the rash behavior and ideas of the red personality.

Still a further point of conflict may arise from the fact that the green personality deeply resents any attempt to change ideas, while the red has a compulsive need to try to influence others.

One area of compatibility which may exist between the two is that both are highly affectionate and emotional. Depending upon the goals of the individuals, this could provide the basis for some type of relationship.

Red-Yellow Combination

While there are some areas of conflict between a red and a yellow personality, this combination could be highly compatible. Both personalities are motivated by a constant desire for change and innovation. Both are attracted to causes and are highly idealistic. Since a yellow personality is highly creative and inclined to dwell in theory, the action-oriented red personality may very well turn the creativity of a yellow partner into great accomplishment.

Between these two energetic personalities, there are several areas of conflict. The yellow personality tends to be shy and hesitant with other people, while the red personality thrives on continuous and extensive social involvement. Even more significant, the yellow personality, whose ideas are very carefully thought out, may become angered at the red personality's quick judgments and impulsive opinions.

Aside from these differences, the many common traits that these two personalities hold can lead to a compatible and stimulating relationship.

Red-Blue Combination

These two basic personalities are highly incompatible. Establishing an intimate and harmonious relationship will be extremely difficult because the basic traits of the red and the blue personality are in conflict in almost every area.

The blue personality is driven by a need for peace, tranquility, and harmony, while the red personality is constantly searching for excitement, variety, and action. The blue is skeptical of strangers and feels uncomfortable outside his or her social group. The red will be constantly forcing the blue into a number of diverse social situations which will make the blue personality extremely uneasy. Basically cautious and conservative, the blue will be appalled by the flamboyant and unconventional actions of the red. The red, refusing to accept any part of a humdrum life, will keep things in constant turmoil through a quest for new experiences. In almost everything, the red personality poses a threat to the harmony and tranquility so necessary to the blue.

A lasting relationship between these two personality types will probably exist only if the blue allows complete domination by the red.

Red-Brown Combination

With rare exceptions, these two personalities will be generally incompatible. A steady, conscientious worker, with strong established views, the brown personality is a creature of habit. Brown will be highly intolerant of the extremes in behavior to which red is inclined. Conversely, the red, who is seeking endless variety in life, will be frustrated by brown's insistence upon a steady and predictable existence.

The brown personality has such a sense of dedication to whatever he or she is involved in that there is a strong probability that the red personality may unconsciously exploit this sense of responsibility. This would bring ultimate resentment on the part of brown. Also, the brown personality's deep-seated need for security at all times will be threatened by the red personality's striving for change and activity.

Should a close relationship exist, there will be a definite need for compromise, in which case the brown personality could offer a stabilizing influence in a relationship which is bound to be rocky, at best.

Red-Purple Combination

In general, these two personalities are compatible, for they have many similar traits. Both have a common attraction to causes, although the purple is usually more passive in actual involvement than is the red. Both are rather temperamental and inclined to be inconsistent in their behavior. However, since the purple personality is quite tolerant, the red personality may find purple fairly easy to live with. Although both are inclined to be egotistical, there are strong physical and mental attractions for each other's endowments. As they respect each other's independence, there could be a stimulating relationship in which each finds security and affection.

Major conflict between these two may be avoided by making sure that they do not compete with each other in any given area. Both naturally seek the spotlight and such conflict could lead to the destruction of an otherwise harmonious relationship.

Red-Black Combination

The red and black personalities generally find themselves to be incompatible. While they are both dissatisfied with the existing state of affairs, red's dissatisfaction stems from a rejection of monotony, while the black personality's dissatisfaction stems from a rejection of *life*. Therefore, black is in constant rebellion against all authority.

The black personality has a compulsion to resist any domination, and the black personality's behavior patterns may be quite devious in an attempt to mask this. For example, the black personality may act greatly dignified, exhibiting an apparent willingness to comply with the environment. Inwardly, however, black seethes with resentment and desires to strike out against the existing order of things. Black will particularly clash with red's naturally energetic leadership unless black can dominate the red personality.

The red personality, on the other hand, is basically an aggressive extrovert who will resist the almost certain attempt at domination by black.

Gray-Gray Combination

This is one of the most highly compatible combinations. A mutual desire to escape from all pressures and involvements leads to a peaceful and secure relationship. Both have tired of the endless struggle and turmoil of life and will find security and refuge in their relationship.

Gray-Green Combination

The gray and green personalities will usually find a level of compatibility. While the green personality will become involved in far more social activity than will the gray, the green will offer the gray a stable and balanced existence. They will give to each other the security of strong affection and loyalty, and there should be few upsets and conflicts to mar this generally harmonious relationship.

Gray-Yellow Combination

Incompatibility will tend to be the rule between these two very different personalities. While the gray personality seeks to escape from the demands of society, the yellow personality rushes headlong into social commitments, particularly those of an idealistic nature. Although there will be few occasions of open conflict, yellow's desire for involvement and commitment would pose a constant threat to the retreating gray personality.

Gray-Blue Combination

This combination of personalities is highly compatible. Both have a basic need for tranquility and a tension-free existence. The conservative and sensitive blue personality is a secure buffer for the gray against any radical upsets from the outside world. The blue will find the steady, even temperament of the gray to be a marvelously complementary personality.

Gray-Brown Combination

The gray and brown personalities are highly compatible. The keen emphasis of the brown upon security and unvarying tradition makes brown an ideal partner for gray. The brown's dislike of any dramatic change in the life pattern and steady reliable character are completely in tune with the gray's pursuit of a trouble-free existence.

Gray-Purple Combination

The gray personality will find little compatibility with the purple. The purple's temperamental behavior and desire to be in the limelight may drag the gray into many unwanted and frustrating situations that will upset gray's harmony of existence. Purple's desire for sociability will run counter to gray's desire for seclusion and non-involvement.

Gray-Black Combination

Gray and black personalities are basically incompatible. The black's powerful drive to master both personal destiny and the surrounding environment is directly opposed to gray's desire to be free of any participation whatever. A continuing relationship will exist only where the black personality is in complete domination.

Green-Green Combination

These two personalities will be exceptionally compatible. Their mutual devotion to the responsibilities of home and community will draw them closely together. Their intelligence and sensitivity to social etiquette will enhance their attraction to each other. Because they are affectionate, loyal, and extremely well-balanced people, they will have few emotional conflicts in their relationship. The relationship should be lasting and harmonious.

Green-Black Combination

On the surface, green and black may present an image of compatibility. The black's public image of dignity and worldliness would be impressive to green's social circles and seemingly in keeping with the social norms so dear to green. At times witty and clever, the black personality may exhibit great sociability.

In private, however, the black personality will be in turbulent opposition to the whole established social order that the green personality holds so sacred. There may be a constant tug of war between these two strong personalities, who seek to dominate each other.

Yellow-Yellow Combination

The creative and artistic drives of the yellow personalities will make each sympathetic to the other's abilities, desires, strengths, and weaknesses. It is upon this basis that a compatible relationship can be founded. Both will have a common objective in striving for a Utopian existence within which there will be a freedom for their individual and creative expression.

Because of their great idealism and tendency toward overindulgence in fantasy, however, it will be necessary for one of the partners to attend to the practical demands of everyday living. A practical existence cannot be based solely upon dreams and visions, however stimulating they may be.

Yellow-Blue Combination

The strong contrast in temperaments of the yellow and blue personalities could lead to conflict and incompatibility. Foremost might be the inability of blue to accept or to understand the moody and sometimes erratic behavior of the yellow personality.

The yellow's strong drive for reform and innovation will be at strong odds with the blue's demand for peace and tranquility. The blue might see the yellow as a threat to his or her conservative objectives, while the yellow may feel frustrated by blue's restrictions.

Yellow-Purple Combination

The many similar personality traits of the yellow and the purple could lead to a high degree of compatibility. Both are inclined to be very artistic and creative and are deeply sympathetic to social causes and reform movements. Unfortunately, both may be lacking an ability to take concrete action. Although highly intellectual and perceptive, they are frequently ineffective in accomplishing their goals.

Temperamentally, they are ideally suited to each other and will find each other's company highly stimulating. The purple's authoritative manner may be the only upsetting element in what should be a mutually rewarding relationship.

Yellow-Black Combination

Although the yellow and black find common cause in their dissatisfaction with the existing order, they will have great difficulty in establishing compatibility unless the yellow allows the black to dominate the relationship. The yellow personality will find great attraction in the dignity and force of the black's rebellion against society. In this they will find mutual satisfaction and a base for a degree of compatibility.

Where yellow attempts to dominate the relationship, however, there will be explosive resistance by the black, which will lead to the relationship's eventual destruction.

Blue-Blue Combination

Since blues have a tremendous attraction and liking for each other, this relationship will be highly compatible. Their mutual demand for both tranquility and a life free from tension will eliminate any threat of disharmony in their lives. Even in disagreement, their sensitivity for the other's feelings should prohibit them from making undue demands upon each other. They will work together conscientiously to achieve common life goals. As long as one blue does not attempt to dominate, the relationship will be most harmonious.

Blue-Brown Combination

A relationship between a blue and a brown personality should be highly compatible. Both place a high value on meeting their duties and responsibilities. Both are extremely conscientious workers and have a strong need for security and harmony in family life. The conservative and cautious approach of both personalities will generally prevent any rash or impulsive actions toward each other. However, since both can be quite stubborn and sometimes opinionated, each will resent any attempt at domination by the other.

Blue-Purple Combination

In general, this combination will be incompatible. The blue's inability to cope with or be sympathetic to the fluctuating temperament of the purple personality will be the source of many conflicts. Further, the blue will be highly impatient with the purple's inconsistent and often indecisive behavior. These traits of the purple are in direct opposition to blue's insistence upon an orderly and predictable existence.

On the other hand, purple may be exasperated by the conservative, restrictive demands of blue. Since they are both inclined to be egotistical, they will clash when points of difference arise.

Blue-Black Combination

The combination of blue and black signifies a highly incompatible relationship. The basic black personality, with its determined rebellion, represents a constant threat to the blue's need for security and tranquility. The strong motivations of blue to uphold and perpetuate the existing order clash dramatically with black's compulsion to destroy the existing scheme of things.

A relationship could exist only where the black dominates the partnership, and even then there would be a continual fear and resentment on the part of the blue personality.

Brown-Brown Combination

A union of two browns will produce a highly compatible relationship. Although they may discover that their reluctance to concede readily and their inclination toward temper flare-ups, stubbornness, and jealousy may cause some difficult moments, their mutual desires for material gains and financial security could be a powerfully uniting force. Their common emphasis on home and family and their devotion to duty will override their differences of opinion. Their steady, reliable characters and their deeply ingrained patterns of living provide a firm foundation for a lasting and successful union.

Brown-Purple Combination

A brown and purple combination will tend to be incompatible because of the clash of their basic personality traits. Brown's devotion to duty may cause the naturally authoritative purple to take unfair advantage. Also, purple's artistic temperament may clash strongly with brown's steady consistent behavior. Brown's stubbornness and intolerance may cause him or her to become highly critical of the impulsive and egotistical behavior of purple. Where brown is dominant, however, there could be a productive, though quarrelsome, relationship.

Brown-Black Combination

The brown and black combination generally will be incompatible. As always, in any relationship where black is involved, black must dominate for the relationship to be a lasting one. In such instances, the steady reliability of brown coupled with the driving force of black can produce significant accomplishment, although it will be at the expense of exploiting the brown personality. Under any other circumstances, brown's stubbornness and devotion to traditional patterns will be at odds with black's drive to upset the existing order of things.

Purple-Purple Combination

A combination of two purple personalities could be either highly compatible or highly incompatible. On the negative side, both are inclined to be vain and egotistical in their creative talents and therefore might easily clash over their individual need to be in the spotlight. Such temperament coupled with their skills in sarcasm could lead to frequent and disastrous quarreling.

On the other hand, should they recognize their common tendencies and acknowledge each other's distinctive capabilities, a strong union for the pursuit of happiness could be established. Such a relationship could be highly compatible and fulfilling for each of them.

Purple-Black Combination

A purple and black combination will present an interesting image to the world, although it will be a lasting relationship only if purple permits black to be dominant. Publicly, whether in business or social life, the purple and black combination will present an image of great dignity and worldliness in their attempts to impress others. In public, they may be highly accomplished and successful.

In private, however, there may be a violent clash between these two very egotistical and domineering personalities. If the tolerant purple allows the black to dominate, the union, though quarrelsome, may persist. Should purple attempt to exercise authority, however, the union will end in bitterness and destruction.

Black-Black Combination

Of all the combinations, this is probably the most incompatible. The black's total rebellion and resistance to domination prevents him or her from participating in any successful union in which he or she is not the master. In those rare circumstances in which two black personalities might unite together for a common cause, a relationship could continue only as long as neither encroached upon the other. Any attempt to do so would result in explosive conflict.

Part II Color Power

How Did It Start? What Does It Mean?

As you are beginning to discover, the accuracy of personality analysis through color is really quite amazing. The colors you prefer and those which you reject are indeed definite indicators of the real you—your innermost goals, feelings, and behavior. Also, the colors which surround you have a definite effect upon your state of mind and your physical and mental well-being. These personal relationships between you and color are universal in terms of meaning and effect and are a link between you and your earliest ancestor. In fact, human reactions to color can be traced to the very earliest generations of the human race, and these reactions may indeed be as primitive and basic as the human need for water, food, and shelter.

The history of color is older than the written history of humanity. The symbolism associated with color has its roots in the relationship among primitive peoples, their struggle for survival, and the natural colors of their environment. Prehistoric and primitive peoples have left evidence of the importance of color in their lives in the artifacts, designs, and primitive forms of communication which have been unearthed by archeologists.

For example, color as a means of expression and communication is evident in the cave paintings of early humans. Ideas, concepts, and events could be portrayed through simply drawn symbols. It was easy to devise a crude symbol to depict a tree—  —or the sun—  — and such symbols carry a universal meaning that is timeless and cuts across all cultures. However, a universal set of symbols to depict such emotions as fear, happiness, serenity, and so on is nearly impossible to design in pictorial form. Color, on the other hand, is adaptable to such expression, and it was color that even in ancient times gave people a mode for expressing their innermost feelings and emotions—the emotions which were too abstract to depict through written symbols. It is these early uses of color employed to convey expressions of the inner self that form the roots of modern color psychology.

The colors used by early peoples were the colors of the natural environment—those which could be seen and be made from the animals, plants, and minerals found in nature. Early peoples were especially sensitive to the colors of the environment, for they relied to a great extent upon color cues to help them survive in a hostile and uninviting environment. Their highly developed color vision aided them in intuitively reacting to subtle differences of color posed by dangerous preying animals that might otherwise be hidden by the natural scheme of their surroundings. Sensitivity to color was also an aid in helping early peoples to identify the sources of food gathered or hunted from the environment.

The fact that color was an important and significant part of such early life helps provide understanding for the historically universal meanings of color to the human organism. It is easy to understand, for example, how the reds, oranges, and yellows came to be associated with energy, life, comfort, and activity and to be identified as the "warm" colors when you realize that these are the colors reflected by both sunlight and fire—the sources of warmth and sustainers of life as humans struggled and huddled together for survival in a cold, dangerous, and life-threatening environment. It is also easy to understand the fear, aversion, emptiness, and evil associated with black—the dark, cold, dangerous night with no fire, no light, no warmth. Night was a time when predators could strike and life could be lost without warning. The further association of the blues and greens with coolness, serenity, and stability is similarly explainable. The coolness of water, of a blade of grass, and of the breeze which appears to emanate from the azure-blue sky is the basis for color-symbol relationships based upon daily experience and observation.

These and other relationships between life, color, and environment provide the basis for the universal and primitive meanings associated with color. Because color was a natural mode for expressing the activities of inner life, it became closely associated with mystical and spiritual forms of early communication and expression which were devoted to explaining human existence and providing a meaningful explanation for life's benefits and disasters.

Since black was associated with the lack of comfort and the lack of human benefits, it was natural that it also came to be a positive symbol for life's adversities, dangers, and disasters. Early humans used black to symbolize the demons, evil spirits, and gods with whom they credited the powers of controlling life's miseries, calamities, and catastrophes, particularly that of death.

Red, on the other hand, being associated with warmth, energy, activity, and happiness, was believed to be useful in discouraging, dispelling, and chasing away evil and destruction and in appealing to the spirits believed to be responsible for life's benefits and blessings.

As a result of these symbolic associations and their natural transfer to communicate expressions of mankind's inner life, color came to be intrinsically intertwined with the mystical, spiritual, and religious aspects of human culture. Further, because the spiritual leader was often also the "medicine or faith healer" of the group, and because illness-disease and life-death are so closely associated, color also became associated with healing and therapy. During early years of human life, the religious and medical aspects of color symbolism were inseparable. In more contemporary times, color has continued to be used for therapeutic purposes outside the spiritual and religious aspects of life. A later section of this book will deal with color and health in greater detail.

Medicine men, faith healers, and magicians wore fetishes, charms, and garments of specific colors. Each color was chosen for a specific purpose which related in some way to its basic universal meaning. Charms were made from the semiprecious and precious stones found in the environment, and these stones were chosen for the *power* believed to lie in their colors, rather than their appeal. As human technology advanced and people became weavers, cloth and yarn and other such materials were dyed various hues from natural materials obtained through animal and plant life and minerals found in the environment, and these added to the array of colored objects which could be used for symbolic purposes.

The colors used for charms and clothing were employed to deal with the spirits and the gods believed to control human destiny and also to prevent and/or treat illness and disease.

Red rubies, bloodstones, garnets, and other materials were used to keep away evil spirits, to prevent natural disasters, and to promote longevity. Red was also an important part of the religious ceremonies of sacrifice which were conducted to appease the gods and the spirits.

Yellow, believed to be the opposite of black, a symbolism probably derived from the relationship between sunlight and darkness, was found in amber, gold, and various plants and flowers. In addition, dyed materials and honey were also chosen because of their yellow color. Yellow was believed to be useful in promoting happiness and prosperity, and because it was believed to be opposite to black, it was also used in rites of sacrifice to appease the spirits of evil.

Green emerald and jade and objects from nature, such as plants, were used to promote strength and fertility and to bring about rain. Green was also used to keep away spirits of an evil nature.

Blue was especially significant because of its relationship to seemingly "heaven-sent" events. Blue sapphires, flowers, robes, and so on were used to deter evil, especially a blue fetish with an "evil eye" painted on it. Blue was believed to have the power to promote all types of virtuous behaviors and was worn to promote faith, obedience, trustworthiness, and so on. It was often used in the attire of faith healers and magicians, as it was believed to have large general powers of mystical and spiritual origin and thus bring consequent benefits to its wearer.

The blue-green of turquoise was similarly believed to have the power to frighten away evil spirits. It was especially significant to the native American cultures of the Southwest, where it was used to treat snake bites, poisonings, and eye diseases.

Purple, being a mixture of energetic red and serene blue, also enjoys a mixture in terms of meaning. Amethysts, flowers, and purple fabrics were often worn by those of esteemed social position, as purple is associated with royalty. It is also associated with mystical and creative phenomena, and was also employed to promote virtuous behavior and to induce pleasant dreams and sleep.

Black in the form of jet, charcoal, coal, animal fur, and so on was used to ward off death. It found a significant place in rites of sacrifice and appeasement in many different cultures.

White, along with yellow, was associated with sunlight and heavenly light, particularly the latter. Since its source was in heaven, it was closely related to the gods and spirits and was used to chase away evil spirits and to provide heavenly protection. Diamonds were especially significant and powerful as objects through which the magic of white could be bestowed.

Color Symbolism in Religion, Philosophy, and Culture

As civilization progressed and spiritual and intellectual life centered around philosophy and organized forms of religions, color symbolism as a means of expressing the inner life of humanity continued to be associated with the spiritual part of life through symbolism in organized sets of beliefs. In addition, the most important color symbols of various religions and cultures tend to be indicative of the "personality" of the particular religion or culture.

Ancient Greece

The ancient Greeks pursued the rediscovery of the "Golden Age" of humankind, a time which they perceived as perfect because of the harmonious relationship between humans and the universe and because of the balance of human virtues in the lives of individuals. To symbolize this sought-after harmony, the Greeks used red, blue, and white. Red stood for sacrifice and love, blue for truth and integrity, and white for purity. These were the human virtues believed necessary for a perfect, harmonious, and balanced life, and individuals wore clothing of red, blue, and white, hoping to attract and develop the appropriate balance of these virtues.

Major Religions

Yellow is an especially significant color to many Eastern religions. It is the most important color associated with Confucius and Buddha, and it is the sacred color of India's Brahmans. Blue is the color associated with Yahweh, the God of Judaism, while green is the primary color symbol of Islam. Both green and blue are important to Christianity, although green seems of greater importance than blue. All these religions also use other colors for specific symbols related to particular rites or beliefs.

Extremely interesting is the relationship between the primary color symbol of each religion and the "personality" characteristics of the religion and/or culture. Religions of the East tend to associate with yellow, the color of openness, activity, movement, and creativity, while religions of the West tend to associate with the more stable and structured blues and greens. Philosophically, Eastern culture and modes of thought may be described as cyclical and open in comparison to Western culture and modes of thought, which are described as straight-line and hierarchical, based upon law, logic, and sequential, rather than cyclical, styles of thinking. While this is an oversimplification, it does offer a basis for the fact that cultural, as well as individual, personality is expressed through color preference. In further support of this notion of cultural color personality indicators is the fact that, although colors have a universal effect upon the human organism—*i.e.*, red is exciting, blue is calming—research shows that there are differences in the order of color preferences exhibited by members of different cultures.

Color Symbolism and Systems of Human Existence

Early humans believed that the earth was the center of the universe. Civilizations which were separated by both geography and time developed systems which described their geographical positions within this earth-centered universe which had certain similarities. The earth was divided into sections, and each section had a function which explained the cause of natural phenomena, and each section was associated with a color symbolic to its position and/or function within the universe. Many of these universe systems included the then-known heavenly bodies—six planets and the moon. The heavenly bodies were of extreme importance because of the association of protection, benevolence, light, and darkness, which was related in some way to the heavens, heavenly light, or the lack of it.

The Navajo culture, for example, described the universe with itself at the center, surrounded by mountains on four sides. The rising and falling mountain slopes and the geographical positions of the mountains were believed to cause day and night. The southern mountains, symbolized by blue, brought dawn; the eastern mountains, symbolized by white, brought daylight; the western mountains caused twilight and were symbolized by yellow; darkness descended from the northern mountains, the symbol being the obvious black.

Early Egyptians also divided the known world into four sections, or areas—the Upper Nile, the Lower Nile, the fields surrounding the Nile, and the heavens. This symbolized the two strongest forces in Egyptian life—the Nile, which was the source of life; and the heavens, which were believed to be the source of spiritual life. The Upper Nile was symbolized by white; the Lower Nile was symbolized by red. This was reflected in the color of the crown which the Pharaoh chose to wear. In Egyptian temples, floors were green to symbolize the green fields of the Nile, and the ceilings were blue, with representations of the constellations, to symbolize the heavens.

Interest in the heavens and devotion to a belief in the divine relationship between the heavens and the meaning of human existence were also shared by many different cultures. A deep-seated inner need of humans to find a meaning for existence in this mystical relationship between heaven, earth, and humankind is clearly evident in the development of systems of astrology.

Astrology is probably the oldest empirical "science" of the human race. It has been significant in Egyptian, Indian, Chinese, Greek, medieval European, and other world cultures throughout the ages. Furthermore, the various systems of astrology that were developed are quite similar in organization and symbolic coding. Although the scientific advances of nineteenth- and twentieth-century research tended to dampen the interest in astrology, especially among the educated populace of the twentieth century, in recent years it has again received renewed attention and interest. Most people are familiar with the basic concept of astrology—the destiny of individual lives being controlled by forces which are in effect in a particular section of the heavens at the time of birth, that there are twelve signs of the zodiac, each with a symbol indicative of its position in the heavenly sphere. However, it is interesting to note that some cultures also assigned a color symbol to each sign. The colors used appear to have a relationship to the "personality" of each sign: for example, Aries, the ram, might be symbolized by red; Cancer, the moon, by silver; Pisces, the fish, by aquamarine—the blue of the sea.

Color Symbolism, Universe Systems, and Architecture

Very young children and very young and primitive cultures tend to react to the stimulus of color only. As maturity increases, in both individuals and cultures, reaction—and, hence, symbolization —is to a combination of color and form. Examples of this growing cultural maturity can be seen in many of the ancient buildings unearthed by archaeologists, particularly those believed to be temples of worship. In such temples, both color and form were combined to symbolize the universe and the meaning of its various parts.

Such a building usually reflected the particular culture's view of the universe. Since the universe was generally believed to be earth-centered and surrounded by seven heavenly bodies, this was incorporated into the architectural design of the building. A building might contain seven architectural components arranged within the larger structure and/or around another component representing the earth. Each component would represent a specific planet or the moon, and each would be decorated with a specific color to symbolize the heavenly body or part of the universe represented. A common symbolism might be black for Saturn, silver or white for the moon, red for Mars, and so on. Position was also reflected symbolically, both in structure, or form, and color. The highest or most important part of the building would represent the moon, or the believed epitome of universal structure conceived by the culture, and the color symbol would be representative of position. Silver, gold, or white were often used to symbolize the most desirable or beneficial aspect of the culture's universe, with black representing the lowest or most undesirable position in the universe.

Color and Health

It is a known fact that color, as embodied in the light waves of sunlight, is necessary for the health and survival of both animals and plants, therefore, the concept that a form of color is essential to human health should be easy to understand and accept. The interesting concept that is not so well known is the power ascribed to color *per se* as a legitimate form of treatment and/or prevention of illness and disease.

As previously stated, primitive cultures and early civilizations held the power of color as crucial when dealing with the gods and spirits believed to control human destiny. Since the intrinsic relationships among health and comfort, illness and calamity, and the special powers of the gods and spirits are understandable, it follows that these relationships led humans to extend color power to the treatment and/or prevention of the diseases and illnesses associated with life's disasters, misfortunes, and calamities.

Choices of colors used for health purposes were based upon environmental factors, plus the accumulated knowledge of observation and experience. Since illness was believed to be a natural part of life, colors used in its treatment were taken from the natural environment. Specific choices were empirically based and related to the impact of the illness upon the color of the skin or human body and to the color inherent in a specific affliction, such as the red of a skin rash or the yellow of jaundice.

Primitive cultures and early civilizations used color for health purposes in a variety of treatments. Certain commonalities did exist among cultures which were separated by both geography and time. The following summary spans numerous centuries and cultures, but identifies those areas which were common to two or more groups. It is interesting from the point of view of the overwhelming consensus shared by diverse peoples in the power of color *per se*. Objects used were those found in nature or materials dyed from natural sources. These objects included stones, jewels, woven materials, and natural animal and plant life, such as blood, fur, insects, and flowers. As such, the colors were essentially color pigments rather than color lights, a differentiation which will be explained in more detail in the next chapter.

Red, the energetic giver of action and comfort, was used in health treatments for pimples, skin rashes, sore throats, smallpox, scarlet fever, convulsions, and male sterility. Note the relationship of the color associated with the illness in the first five disorders, and the relationship between the universal ennervating effect of red to the need for stimulation in the last two disorders.

Yellow was used for a variety of treatments. Some of these were based upon the yellow-black opposite association made by early peoples. Jaundice, liver-related ailments, earaches, ulcers, boils, blindness, goiter, and fevers were treated with yellow. It was also used to prevent miscarriages and as an antidote to poisoning. The relationships between the color and the illness is not so clear here as with red, but some are apparent. For example, the yellow of jaundice and infectious pus are associations by color. The relationship of yellow by symbolism is less apparent.

Green was used in the treatment of sunstroke, eye diseases, indigestion, water retention, and some skin problems. It was also employed to curtail hemorrhages, particularly in the case of childbirth.

Blue was used as a general treatment along with others of a more specific nature. This probably stemmed from the belief in blue as a power of heavenly quality, associated with the benevolence of the gods and spirits in general.

Contemporary Uses of Color in Health Treatment

The use of color as a remedy for illness and disease is not only historical, it has continued through the ages and was especially popular among certain groups of medical practitioners during the eighteenth and nineteenth centuries. It is still relied upon by some members of the medical profession today, although there is wide disagreement between those who support its use and those who believe color to be ineffective as a treatment *per se*. However, color is a significant cue to diagnosing the state of an individual's health. The yellow of jaundice, various colorations surrounding the eyes associated with specific diseases, and general coloration of healthy skin are among color cues used by doctors for first-line indicators of possible illnesses. Additional uses of color in medical treatment which are generally agreed upon lie in the use of X-ray and ultraviolet treatments. These in essence are "color" treatments when one realizes that each specific color is simply light waves of a specific length. X-ray and ultraviolet light fit that description, although they are light waves which cannot be seen by the human eye. In addition, there is more general professional consensus on the use of color, both pigment and light, in the treatment of various forms of mental illness. This type of treatment is directly related to the universal effects of color upon the human organism—*i.e.*, red is exciting, blue is calming, and so on.

Less known is the fact that color *per se* has been, and continues to be, used in the treatment of various human afflictions. While there is wide disagreement within the medical profession about the efficacy of its use, those practitioners who do employ color in treatment do so on the basis of the evidence of experience and success. In contrast to the ancient use of color in health treatment, contemporary application is more likely to be in the form of light rather than pigment. Also, modern applications of color are based upon the effect of the color upon the human organism, rather than upon the magical power of color.

The following general summary is provided as a matter of interest to tempt individual curiosities into further study. It is quite general, omitting specific details necessary to professional application. It is not a do-it-yourself guide to self-treatment or self-cure and should not be used as a medical handbook. If ill, consult your physician.

RED is used in the treatment of rheumatism, poor circulation, low blood pressure, eczema, paralysis, and male impotency. It is used to increase the emotional reactions and to excite individuals who are mentally depressed.

BLUE, which appears to have an opposite effect on the human organism to red, is used to treat sunstroke, infections, burns, cuts, headaches, diarrhea, and high blood pressure. It is applied to individuals who exhibit tension, irritability, and hysteria.

GREEN, which is a mixture of blue and yellow, is used less often than other colors. It has been applied in the treatment of high blood pressure and such conditions of an emotional nature as anxiety, shell shock, and neurosis.

VIOLET, or purple, is used to treat insomnia and headaches. It appears to have a calming effect when used with individuals who are extremely irritable or nervous. It is also suggested as a treatment for low sexual activity in females.

YELLOW is a stimulant, less intense than red or orange. It has also been used in the treatment of constipation, heartburn, and disorders of the lungs. It is used in the treatment of liver-related illnesses.

ORANGE induces some increase in blood pressure and stimulates the emotions, but is less intense in its effects than is red. In addition, orange has a pleasant association with food and appears to enhance the appetite.

Combinations of colors are also used in the treatment of several illnesses and diseases.

Because of its association with mysticism, spiritualism, phenomenon of a sensual nature, and artistic—as compared to scientific—endeavor, color is not widely accepted as a proven source of health treatment. However, when one realizes the close relationship between physical and mental health and simultaneously considers the impact of color on the human psyche, it is not unreasonable to at least suggest that color as therapy has some logical base. Further, it seems that organized and scientific research to establish either the efficacy or the foolishness of color as treatment, certainly has a place in the medical profession.

More About Color: Science, Psychology, Application

A comprehensive understanding of color should include information from three areas:

1. The scientific structure and properties of color
2. The symbolism of color as it relates to color preference and color effect
3. The application of color to such practical matters as advertising and sales, safety, business efficiency and communication, and interior decoration

Information on the scientific nature of color and its properties should include an understanding of traditional, as compared to contemporary, theories of color harmony. Both are inextricably intertwined with the social-cultural aspects of the historical eras in which they received acknowledgment and popularity, and both are important in the development of a sound understanding of the practical applications of color to everyday life. This information provides food for the imagination, as well as a necessary tool for the organized and creative applications of color to various aspects of everyday life. Further, knowledge of the physical properties of color gives additional insight into the symbolic meanings and effects of color relative to both personality and application.

The Science of Color

There is no one organized body of knowledge that actually falls under the umbrella of "color science." Information about the structure and properties of color is actually derived from research and information gleaned from many different fields or disciplines. Much information evolves from the discipline of biology which deals with color adaptation of the various species, color embellishment for mating purposes, and color blindness and color weakness. Other information is available from the physical sciences and visual arts. The information which follows is derived mostly from the latter two fields of knowledge.

There are four basic factors involved in the perception, identification, and personal reaction to color. They are: light, hue, saturation, and brightness. Light is probably the least thought of, but the most important of, these factors. For without light there would be no color for two separate, but related, reasons.

First, without the presence of either natural or artificial light, it would be impossible to perceive differences in color. An example of this can be seen in the fact that in a closet without light, it is often difficult to determine differences in the color of clothing, particularly those garments which are similar in shade or color. Further, if you were to stand inside the closet and close the door, you would be in darkness and differences in color would be completely indistinguishable.

Second, the reason this is true is that any specific color perceived, such as red, is actually the reflection of the light waves of a specific length. Pure "white" light, or sunlight, is made up of a spectrum of light waves which contain all the colors perceptible to the human eye, as well as those which cannot be "seen." When you see a red dress, for example, you are seeing cloth which reflects red light and absorbs the light waves of all other colors. White is a reflection of all light waves; black is the absorption of all light waves or colors. The absorbed light waves contain energy which becomes part of the object. This is the reason, for example, that a house with a black roof will be much hotter inside than a house with a light-colored roof. This phenomenon of the spectrum of color contained within sunlight can be demonstrated through a simple experiment with which most elementary school children are familiar. A prism held up to the light will receive sunlight on one side. The light waves will be separated and emerge from the prism as illustrated on the following page.

When you see a rainbow, you are seeing a natural example of the above effect. The earth's atmosphere has behaved as a prism and separated the light waves going through it into the varied colors of the rainbow.

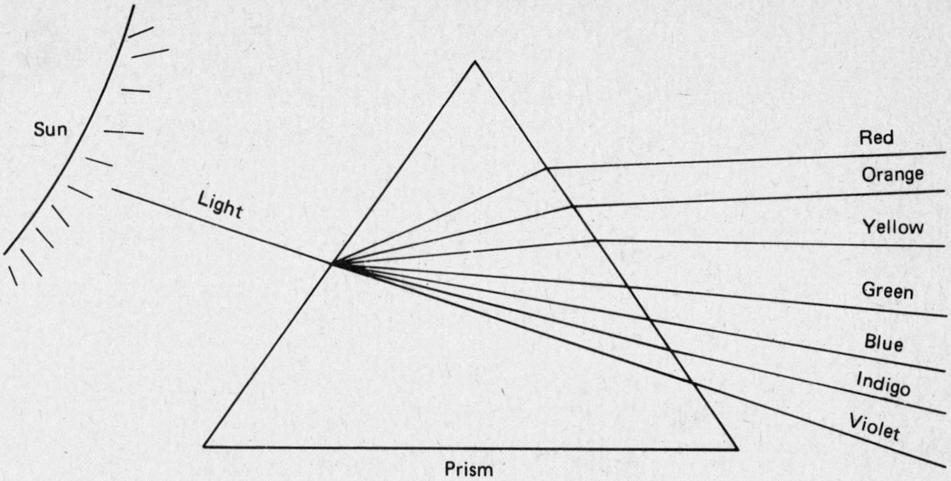

The second factor involved in color perception is the one with which most people are familiar—hue. Hue is the display of a specific color, such as red, or yellow, or blue. The third factor, saturation, is more complex. It is determined by the depth and strength of the color, or by the lack of depth and strength. In terms of depth, the color may be a tint—pastel blue—or a shade—dark blue. Strength is displayed by whether the color is strong or is washed out.

Brightness, the fourth factor, is displayed through clarity and intensity. An example of this can be seen in the comparison of a bright "fire-engine" red to a more muddied or subdued "barn-red."

When you react to color, you are reacting to a complex and often subtle combination of these factors. When you react to color by expressing a preference, you are reacting to the above factors plus the factor of the specific array from which you may select. For example, an individual who names blue as his or her favorite color might indeed choose a different hue as a first choice if the blue provided in the set from which to choose is too dark, too washed out, or too bright in relation to the other colors.

Color Theory: Mixture and Harmony

Traditional theories of color lend an understanding to color mixture and color harmony that is useful when applying color psychology to everyday life. When discussing color mixture, it is necessary to differentiate between pigment and light, for the basics are somewhat different.

When you perceive the colors in the rainbow or the colors separated by the prism, you are perceiving color light. When you perceive the colors in clothing, on the printed page, in paintings, on walls, and so on, you are seeing or perceiving color pigments. When dealing with the mixture of colored light, such as in theater lighting or in your color-TV set, there are three primary colors: red, *green*, blue. Your color-TV set, for example, has three color guns or a three-in-one gun and contains a blue, green, and a red component. All other colors are made from appropriate mixtures of these three primary colors. When all three are combined, the result is white.

However, when dealing with color pigments, such as paints, chalks, inks, and so on, the three primary colors are red, *yellow*, and blue. The information which follows is based upon principles of pigment mixtures. If you are interested in the mixture of colored lights, you must remember that the primary *green* light performs the same function as the primary *yellow* pigment. For example, a mixture of green and red light would produce orange, but a mixture of red and yellow pigment would produce an orange hue.

Traditional color theory is based upon the relationship of three primary colors—red, yellow, and blue, on a two-dimensional color wheel. This model provides information on hue only. Contemporary three-dimensional models in the shapes of pyramids and cones can be located which provide information on brightness and saturation, as well as hue.

The two-dimensional color wheel shows the relationships of color pigments in two ways: complements or opposites on the wheel, and the results of mixing adjacent colors on the wheel. As stated, the three basic or primary colors are red, yellow, and blue.

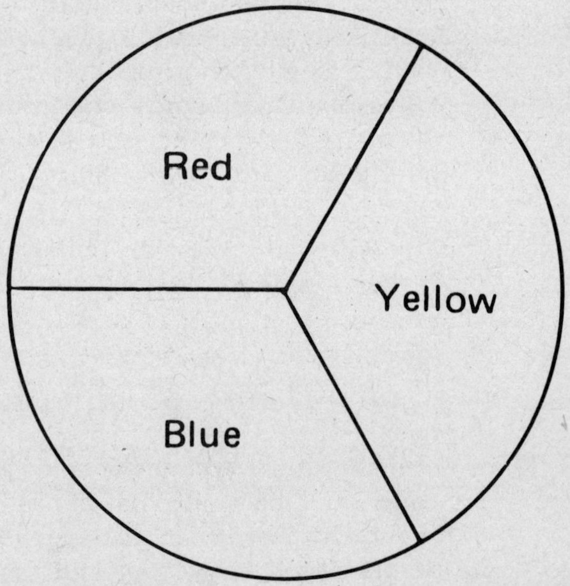

The three secondary colors are orange, green, and purple. These are made by mixing adjacent primary colors: red + yellow = orange; yellow + blue = green; blue + red = purple. When all three primary pigments are combined, the result is black.

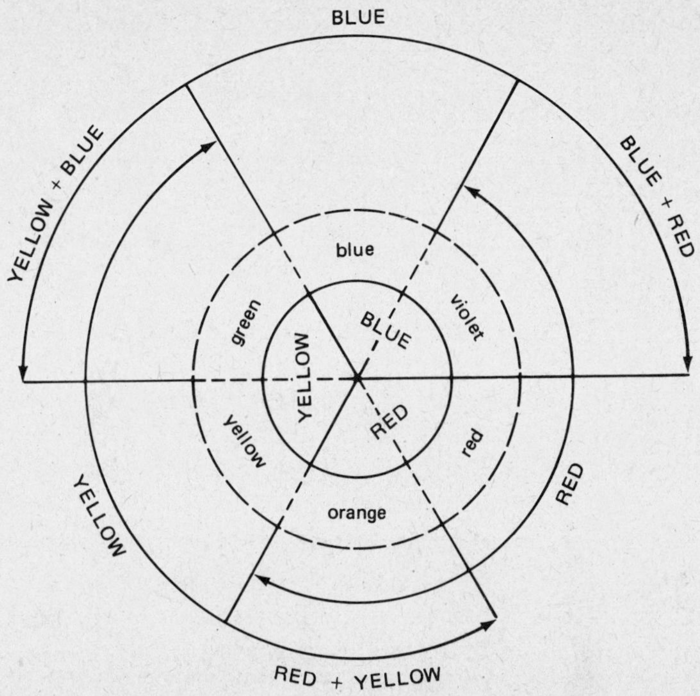

Complementary colors, or opposites, fall opposite each other on the color wheel—*i.e.*, red-green, orange-blue, yellow-purple. Note that complements are always a warm-cool combination. Color complements, when mixed together in the proper amounts, will always produce gray. They nullify each other and the result is a "non-color." The relationship of this physical property of the color gray to its psychological properties in terms of "non-involvement" should be obvious. Psychological properties of other secondary colors also take into account the physical properties of the two primary colors from which each is made. Green is a stable mixture of cheerful, active yellow and serene, quiet blue. Purple is a mixing of exciting, active red, and calm, tranquil blue. In both cases, the personality descriptors reflect this through characteristics of an energetic character combined with characteristics of a quieter or more retiring character.

Traditional theories of color harmony were based upon the position and relationship of colors on the wheel. Certain combinations were believed harmonious, while other combinations were definitely not harmonious. Complements, for instance were harmonious, while adjacent colors were considered non-harmonious. Also considered harmonious were trios of color whose positions on the color wheel could be projected into an equilateral triangle and sets of four colors whose positions on the wheel could be projected into a square, rectangle, or other congruous four-sided figure. The traditional rules of color harmony were quite structured, even rigid, and other combinations were considered unacceptable.

However, contemporary views of color harmony are quite different and are related to the freedom and flexibility of expression associated with the decade of the 1960s. Theories of color harmony are now much more flexible, relaxed, and based on a sort of "anything goes, if it is personally pleasing" basis. Thus, you may choose colors for your home and your apparel which are pleasing combinations to you without concern over their propriety or acceptance by others.

More About Color and Personality

As you should now realize, individual reaction to color is quite spontaneous and uninhibited, therefore quite indicative of basic emotions and attitudes which individuals may intentionally or unintentionally suppress under testing conditions of greater formality and verbalization. Because such reactions are uninhibited, they tell a great deal about a person's inner life—that part which is unknown or hidden from the individual and which lies in the unconscious mind.

Further, color preferences are also revealing relative to the individual's level of inhibition or openness *per se*. Open, extroverted people tend to choose the warm colors and brighter, clearer tones of the cool colors, while inhibited and introverted individuals tend to choose the blues and greens, gray and muddied, subdued, washed-out tones of the warmer colors.

Color choices are also indicative of the developmental level or maturity of the individual and usually change as a person grows into adulthood. Generalizations drawn from this basic principle, however, are much more flexible today than two decades ago, when maturity was believed to be definitely present when an individual chose cool colors and pastels or shades, while immaturity was linked to the choice of bright and vibrant colors. Young children tend to choose colors which are bright and basic and highly saturated. Purple is a favorite choice of adolescents and is quite indicative of typical adolescent emotional, physical, and mental turmoil and the often undeveloped or questioning attitudes of adolescence toward self-concept and ego fulfillment. However, the adult who prefers choices of bright basic colors and of hues of purple category is better described as "child-like," rather than immature, from a positive point of view. Such choices are more likely to be characteristic of creative, artistic, original, problem-solving persons whose inherent creativity requires a child-like approach to life tasks in terms of openness, curiosity, and flexibility in order to make their creativity functional and productive.

Color preferences not only change over a period of years, but they are also affected by mood and particular circumstances of the situation or particular time in which they are made. This means that if you are somewhat depressed or life is posing difficulties, your tendency to choose the cooler colors in preference to the warmer colors is more likely. Or it may simply alter the order of preference. The reverse is true during times of joy, happiness, and enthusiasm. Your tendency to choose the brighter, warmer colors is more likely.

The following table is a summary of indicators of color in terms of both effect and reaction and is highly indicative of the basic personality.

types which would choose each color. Information from this summary may be used in combination with furthering your understanding of color psychology and be applied to the information in the next section on applied uses of color to everyday life.

RED: *Symbolic and personality descriptors*: adventurous, fast, exciting, hot, vivid, restless, loud, energetic, active, direct, dominant, autonomous, fiery, impulsive, full, self-confident, aggressive, extroverted, strong, enervating, intense
Emotional descriptors: passion, love, achievement, hate, anger
Other: creates illusion of weightiness and extended time
Symbolic sources: fire, blood

ORANGE: *Symbolic and personality descriptors*: bright, charming, active, noisy, glowing, luminous, cheerful, jovial, hilarious, sociable, exuberant, energetic, forceful
Emotional descriptors: sociability, cheer, exuberance
Other: pleasantly associated with appetite and food; also associated with autumn
Symbolic sources: fire, sunlight. It is similar to, but less intensive than red in its effect upon people.

YELLOW: *Symbolic and personality descriptors*: free, changeable, healthy, open, loose, sunny, radiant, happy, spontaneous, imaginative, artistic, intellectual, receptive, sociable, innovative, eye-catching, radiant, moving, prosperous, energetic, warm, self-development
Emotional descriptors: idealism, happiness, sociability
Symbolic sources: sunlight, fire

GREEN: *Symbolic and personality descriptors*: stable, orderly, fertile, balanced, solid, natural, cool, clear, peaceful, refreshing, focused, earthly, quiet, moist, meditative, concentrated, enduring, self-respectful
Emotional descriptors: persevering, tenacious, constant, selective, dignified
Other: indicative of an active inner life
Symbolic source: green plant life

BLUE: *Symbolic and personality descriptors*: dignified, harmonious, poised, rational, loyal, trustworthy, contented, tranquil, serene, subdued, virtuous, passive, cold, ethical, slow, wet, organized, relaxed, balanced, self-centered
Emotional descriptors: melancholy, contemplative, tractable
Symbolic sources: sky, water

PURPLE: *Symbolic and personality descriptors*: deep, soft, misty, artistic, mystical, pompous, regal, magical, dreamy, unique, splendid, cool, mournful, sensitive, enchanting, majestic, talented, shadowy, self-concerned, self-identification
Emotional descriptors: moody, temperamental, aloof, sensitive, lonely
Symbolic source: more difficult to define in an environmental context; perhaps the mixture of red energy and blue tran-

quility which results in hard-to-define mysterious qualities of shadowy images

BROWN: *Symbolic and personality descriptors*: earthy, sensuous, healthy, vital, easy, comforting, rich, secure, habitual, reliable, dutiful, self-accepting
Emotional descriptors: reliable, secure
Symbolic source: brown earth—dirt—and its vital relationship to the source of food

GRAY: *Symbolic and personality descriptors*: concealing, non-involving, quiet, peaceful, neutral, middle, average, dull, separate, calm, conservative, self-concealing
Emotional descriptors: reflective, passive
Symbolic source: nullifying effect of mixing color complements

BLACK: *Symbolic and personality descriptors*: dark, somber, evil, dignified, mysterious, mournful, empty, depressing, deadly, ominous, negative, deathly, extinctional, nothingness
Emotional descriptors: regression, withdrawal, rebelliousness, dissatisfaction
Symbolic source: night

WHITE: *Symbolic and personality descriptors*: pure, clean, cold, heavenly, bright, light, good, innocent, holy, clear, natural, balanced
Emotional descriptors: frank, moral
Symbolic source: light (opposite of night)

Practical Application of Color

Since color is known to have specific and significant effects upon human beings, it is only logical that this knowledge, combined with information on the science and theory of color, should and can be applied to everyday situations in order to promote desired attitudes, human productivity, and preferable results in human behavior. Such application of color is referred to as *functional color*. The term *functional color* clearly identifies the place of color in applied situations—it serves an identifiable purpose or function.

The functional use of color is based upon principles and generalizations derived from color psychology, science and theory of color, field and experimental research, and the results of practical experience. These principles allow a person to use color for specific purposes with predictable outcomes, while incorporating the creativity of using color for aesthetic purposes, as well.

The following are but a few of the wide practical applications of color that are possible in today's complex society.

Advertising

Research indicates that functional color is significant as applied to advertising. Magazine ads which are black-and-white tend to produce better results than similar ads done in four-color, particularly if the company or product is unknown. Four-color magazine ads enhance the image and reputation of established companies and product lines. Large ads are more effective than small ads, but a full-page ad is not necessarily twice as effective as a half-page ad. However, in direct-mail advertising, color is more effective than is black-and-white if there is high contrast between the message and the background.

Offices and Businesses

In offices and businesses, the colors used for interior decoration and office machines need to be selected with employee function in mind. For example, a room used by artists, writers, or people producing new and creative ideas is more conducive to the desired results if bright and warm colors are used. In areas where employees are engaged in routine clerical tasks, cooler, lighter neutral hues are more effective in promoting steady and continuous production. Equipment, such as typewriters, are best if colors are soft and neutral so as not to be distracting. Contemporary colors for such machines often include shades or tints of blue, red, and green, which are more cheerfully motivating than the black, gray, and beige machines so often used in the past.

Waiting Rooms and Reception Areas

Waiting rooms and reception areas need to be decorated to induce attitudes and feelings conducive to the successful client interaction necessary for the particular business or service. For example, a consumer complaint bureau would probably find the stabilizing and calming effects of blues and greens helpful in easing the tensions, anxieties, and angers probably felt by waiting clients.

A doctor's waiting room is similarly filled with persons who are feeling both tension and anxiety, and these are usually combined with feelings of illness and/or physical pain. A scheme similar to the above, which utilizes blues and greens, would be useful in relieving anxiety, while accents of a warmer color, such as yellow, would promote additional attitudes of cheer and health.

A business or service, such as a real estate agency, which hopes to encourage clients to take positive action, would probably find reception or conference areas which emphasize the reds and yellows to be more productive than areas with emphasis on the cool, calm, quiet colors.

Industry

Manufacturing plants have traditionally used gray or beige for machinery and walls to reduce distraction caused by moving parts. A brighter color applied to machine parts or facility hazards may be used to remind workers to use caution around that area or section. The large expanses of neutral colors also reduce the possibilities of confusion and error and make depressing dirt less noticeable. Areas for employee recreation might be decorated in warmer, brighter, more cheerful colors in order to counteract the possibly depressing effect of the grays and beiges.

Education

Although children like, or respond favorably to, and are motivated by bright and cheerful colors, traditional schools of the past were decorated on the same principles as the factory to reduce distraction and confusion. However, it is possible to apply principles of color which will achieve goals of reduced distractibility and confusion while still allowing the use of more interesting colors which will appeal to children. Warm tints combined with bright and colorful accents will promote productivity, motivation, and more cheerful attitudes.

Similarly, publishers of educational textbooks and supplemental materials traditionally used color somewhat sparingly, and then too often the choices were muddied, unsaturated hues of green, brown, and dirty yellow, which were not only uninviting, but entirely unmotivating and quite negative in the area of attitude. Contemporary color theory, however, has made real inroads into the graphics used for educational materials. Colorful media and textbook illustration and design are becoming the rule rather than the exception. Such materials are greatly productive in securing learners' attentions and motivating youngsters to become actively involved in the desired learning activities.

Safety and Public Communications

Public protection and safety services have always relied heavily upon color to support and achieve their respective goals. Yellow school buses are easily spotted, as are yellow or red fire engines. Police vehicles generally are painted with the principle of contrast in mind, although choices of specific colors vary. Red is the traditional indicator of danger; yellow of caution; white of health services. Traffic signs are often done in black and yellow and/or other colors, but rely heavily upon the principle of contrast. In fact, any communication device that requires an intuitive or quick response is best designed if the color, as well as the form, is given careful consideration. This is true because the human response to color is intuitive, while the human response to form is one which is learned.

The foregoing are examples of the almost limitless practical applications of color. In using color for functional purposes, it is important to be aware of certain basic principles.

1. The blues and greens and certain blue-heavy mixtures in the purple-violet range are generally identified as cool colors. These colors have a quieting, stabilizing, and tranquilizing effect upon people. However, large expanses of purple-violet tend to have the opposite effect.

2. The reds, oranges, and yellows are identified as warm colors. Certain red-heavy mixtures in the violet-purple range also fall into this category. These colors are generally exciting, attention-getting, and promote productivity and creativity.

3. Neutral colors, particularly shades and tints of gray, are recessive, unnoticeable, and have little emotional effect upon the people nearby. However, the overuse of such colors in large barren areas where there is little activity can have an extremely dull and boring effect.

4. Contrast is extremely important as an attention-getting device. Black on white, for example, provides high contrast, while orange on yellow provides very little contrast, although the colors themselves have been identified as attention-getting. To apply these principles, the following example will be of help. If one is interested in attracting attention from a distance to a specific location, the orange-yellow combination might be quite successful. However, if one is interested in focusing attention upon a printed message, the contrast principle would provide better results.

5. The use of more than three colors in any one area or integrated color scheme is generally confusing and distracting and creates inner reactions of purposelessness and anxiety.

6. Color blindness and color weakness have not been discussed previously. These handicaps exist in an extremely minute portion of the population, and more often in men than in women. Color weakness—the inability to discriminate all the basic primary and secondary colors—is the more prevalent of the two. Most persons who have a color weakness cannot discriminate between hues of yellow and blue. Persons who are color blind are unable to perceive any hues; however, they often receive cues from other indicators, such as intensity, position, and form. When applying functional color to situations of safety and public communication, it is therefore necessary to employ principles of color psychology combined with the principle of contrast, position, and form. Note, for example, that on red and green stoplights, the position of the colors is generally universal, and on public information signs the contrast between the message and the background is high.

7. The ability to discriminate differences in color increases from infancy through early adulthood, then tends to decrease with advancing age. Senior citizens, for example, are less able to discriminate between similar hues, particularly those of the softer tints, than persons of a younger age.

8. Color can be used to create illusions of space-form relationships. Large expanses of one color can be used to create a more spatial feeling in an area which is quite small and/or broken. Application of more than one color can be used to provide focus on individual areas in an oth-

erwise large and unbroken expanse of space. Cool colors in light tones provide greater space illusion, while brighter tones of the warm colors and darker shades of deeply saturated cool colors provide smaller space illusion.

9. Contemporary theories of color harmony being quite open and flexible place a new meaning on *neutral* as applied to color. While traditionalists would think only in terms of grays, beiges, creams, and so on, contemporary color theorists would support the idea that any color might conceivably be used as a neutral one if the following conditions were met: there is an appropriate balance of brightness, saturation, and contrast against the selected neutral background and that the purpose of the setting is properly considered. For example, a shade or tint of orange might be quite appropriate for restaurant use, but it would be disastrous in a factory area of assembly-line systems or moving machine parts.

10. People who live in drab, colorless, and/or deprived surroundings usually react quite favorably to commercial displays and architectural combinations of color form which are warm, colorful, bright, and comfortably open. Those who live in conditions of affluence and/or rich and varied surroundings tend to react favorably to more traditional, subdued, more sophisticated and cool displays and architectural color-form combinations.

11. Generally, men tend to react more favorably to reds, while women tend to prefer blues.

12. Children prefer bright and basic colors, reacting to color at very young ages, then to realistic combinations of color and form in the pre-adolescent years.

Summary

You and color—an inseparable and exciting combination! Knowing more about the history, psychology, theory and science of color, and of its applications will indeed add exciting new dimensions to your life. Acquiring new awareness, openness, and sensitivity to color will also foster the development of your innate creativity. You have already accomplished both these through the information and involvement provided by this book.

Color can be an honest reflection of the most sensitive and honest "you." Use it to express yourself in your home, your clothing, and your work. Use it also to gain a new understanding of self—an understanding which will enable you to deal with yourself and with others in more direct, honest, creative, and effective ways.

The simplified but revealing information contained in this book may have whetted your color appetite. Indeed, if it has, pursue the subject with conviction, interest, and energy. A mastery of the principles involved in color psychology and color application is a tool which will enable you to gain creative control over yourself and your environment.

Part III Your Color Quotient

Testing Your Color Sensitivity

You may want to refresh your memory by rereading the personality profiles and compatibility indicators before putting your knowledge of color to a test. Once you feel confident in your newly gained understanding of color, proceed to the simulations, games, and social situations which follow.

Although this is described as a test, it is not a standardized test and will not provide a true color quotient, as an intelligence test will produce an intelligence quotient, or I.Q. It will tell you, on a percentage basis, how well you have mastered the simplified information and principles which have been described in this book.

It is actually fun to do and quite entertaining. In fact, you might want to use the games and simulations as a series of party games which can be introduced to any group which has a basic knowledge of color and its relationship to personality analysis. Another possibility is to use the color personality test as an ice-breaker, and then play the games designed to test your knowledge about color. To do this, it might be necessary to make a copy of the first-color-choice personality profiles for use while playing the games. Unless the group is one of close friends with well-established relationships, however, it is probably wise not to become involved in compatibility indicators in a social setting, since this guide is general, not a set of absolute or rigid rules.

The games and simulations which follow will allow you to both test and apply your knowledge of color. Once you begin, finish all the exercises without referring to other sections of the book. When finished, turn to page 57 to find the correct or best answers for the items included.

Section One: Personality

A. This problem tests your knowledge of the eight basic personality types. First, read the personality descriptions listed under Column A, then match each description to one of the colors listed under Column B. Write the appropriate letters in the spaces provided next to the colors.

Column A	**Column B**
a. A good citizen and respectable neighbor; concerned with social etiquette	Red________
b. Desires complete quiet and seclusion; reluctant to become involved	Blue________
c. Steady and reliable; a home and family person	Brown________
d. Impulsive and energetic; craves variety and action	Yellow________
e. Idealistic and creative; shy and aloof	Purple________
f. Conservative and conscientious; hates disharmony	Black________

g. Sensitive, temperamental, and tolerant; inclined to be egotistical Gray__________

h. Rebellious and defiant; wishes to be master of own destiny Green__________

B. Fill in the name of the appropriate color to best answer or complete the following problems.

1. Your local bank has an opening for the position of Bank Manager. The committee has interviewed three persons with excellent qualifications. The committee incidentally discovers that the first applicant prefers yellow, the second prefers green, and the third prefers black. Which do you think will make the best bank manager?

____

2. The local school board has just proposed a bond issue for the purpose of building a new school in the district. The proposal has been presented to a local committee of taxpayers. The discussion that follows is lively and controversial as each committee member presents a personal point of view.

a. Mary Smith thinks the new proposal will be an outstanding example of modern architecture and will add to the aesthetic uplifting of the whole community.

Mary Smith is probably a ____________personality.

b. John Willis makes a dramatic and fiery plea to his fellow taxpayers to support their local school board in improving the education of the community's schoolchildren. John pounds the desk and aggressively punctuates his remarks with energetic movements of his hands and body.

John Willis is probably a ____________personality.

c. Sally O'Toole feels that Mr. Willis, the energetic speaker, has let himself be carried away. She points out that the new bond issue will make necessary an increase in taxes and that it will be foolhardy to act impulsively or rashly on such a matter. She feels that the present facilities are quite adequate.

Sally O'Toole is probably a ____________personality.

d. George Stone, when called upon to give his opinion, is most reluctant to commit himself or to become involved in a discussion of the issue. It is obvious that he would prefer to not even be there.

George Stone is probably a ____________personality.

3. On a flight between Los Angeles and Chicago, two hijackers with drawn weapons, using a female passenger as a hostage, burst into the pilot's cabin and confront the pilot, co-pilot, and navigator. They announce their intention to take over the plane and divert the aircraft to Cuba. They assure the crew that any effort at resistance will result in the death of the hostage.

a. The pilot calmly assures the hijackers of his cooperation. While gravely concerned, he is anxious to maintain a calm atmosphere since he realizes that rash action on the part of the crew might trigger a violent and dangerous reaction from the hijackers. As in all other problematic situations, he realizes that a calm, rational approach is the most logical course to pursue.

The pilot is probably a ____________personality.

b. The co-pilot is angered by such stupid and irresponsible action on the part of the hijackers. He has a deep feeling of contempt for the crude and unsophisticated hijackers. He is certain that they can be outwitted and makes little attempt to hide his sarcasm. Despite his anger, however, he takes no positive action, preferring to leave that to others.

The co-pilot is probably a ____________personality.

c. The navigator is immediately outraged for having been pushed into a situation beyond his control. His immediate reaction is to lash out at the hijackers and destroy them despite the danger to himself and to the others aboard the plane. A look from the pilot, however, stops him, but he secretly determines that he will strike, if and when the opportunity presents itself.

The navigator is probably a ____________personality.

d. While the hostage is both concerned for her own and the others' safety, and feels quite indignant about the impropriety of the situation, she is secretly pleased at being the center of attention.

She is probably a ____________personality who has an unsatisfied need for recognition, as shown by her rejection of ____________.

e. The hijackers are both rebellious and angry about the conditions in their present life. However, they are both hopeful of finding a new and better life in Cuba.

They are probably ____________personalities whose goals in life are reflected by a second color choice of ____________.

C. In the following situations, determine the first and second color choice indicators of the personalities described. Remember, the first choice indicates behavior, and the second color choice indicates goals.

1. A citizen's committee has been formed to prepare a report to the city council on the best way to use an endowment of $500,000 which has been left to the city by a former resident. The endowment is very general, stipulating only that the money be used for a project that helps or enhances the lives of the community's residents.

a. With flair and imagination, Sara Lyons proposes a new modern building for a cultural center devoted to the visual and performing arts, with a library-media center in which citizens of all ages can pursue self-study. Sara already sees herself in the role of center director, where she can gain recognition and have a major influence on the lives of many people.

Sara is probably a ____________-____________ personality.

b. Lance Wills excitedly and enthusiastically proposes the construction of an adult athletic stadium with facilities for indoor sports and physical exercise. When someone suggests that this type of facility would neither serve the community's youth nor many handicapped or senior citizens, Lance becomes enraged. He sees no other alternative to his proposal and cannot deal with other people who try to change, dominate, or control his ideas or life-style.

Lance is probably a ____________-____________ personality.

c. Grace Drake quietly suggests that the committee consider a more financially conservative approach. Rather than putting the largest share of the money into a new and expensive building, she suggests that the committee support the establishment of a community orchestra and provide money for a regular concert series over a period of five years. At the end of that time, if the community has shown interest and support, the committee should consider building a permanent facility. Grace is a soloist with an out-of-town group and has imagined the lights and enchantment of performing on a regular basis. Besides, it would be a lot more convenient if she didn't have to drive so far in order to participate with the group.

Grace is probably a ____________-____________ personality.

d. Steve Burns doesn't know why he was even asked to participate on the committee. He would much prefer retiring to the comfort and security of his home at the end of the day. Besides, he hasn't had a good or an original idea since he was nine and wanted to build a dog house for the family pet. He had nothing to propose to the group until yesterday, when he asked his wife to jot down a few notes while she was making out the shopping list. Using his wife's notes, Steve rises and detachedly suggests the committee consider a tree-planting program to enhance the streets, parks, and Big Basket Supermarket (Steve turned the paper over and inadvertently started to read the grocery list). He mumbles an apology and takes his seat with a sigh of relief.

Steve is probably a ____________-____________ personality.

Section Two: Compatibility

1. Terri Jones and Greg Ball are taking a neighborhood group of six youngsters to the zoo. They are going to divide the children into two groups and each will supervise one of the small groups. By playing a game with the children, Terri and Greg have found the following color preferences for themselves and the children: Terri—yellow; Greg—brown; John—green; Tom—red; Sue—blue; Ann—purple; Pam—gray; Doug—black. On the basis of color compatibility, arrange the above people into two groups.

Group A	**Group B**
Terri—yellow	Greg—brown
a.____________	d.____________
b.____________	e.____________
c.____________	f.____________

g. Which group do you think will be easier to supervise? Why?

____

h. Which youngster might pose the most difficulty in a group situation?

____

2. Jerry Dawson, manager of the XYZ Dating Service, has the personality profiles of six applicants on his desk and is attempting to match them for a first introduction. First, read the personality profiles and determine each applicant's basic personality. Then match the applicants on the basis of color compatibility.

a. Jean Harris is a sensitive, conservative person who describes herself as loyal, sincere, and conscientious. Jean likes to surround herself with cool colors and classical music and finds the possibility of a new and unknown relationship rather upsetting. She accompanied a friend to XYZ and filled out the application only because the secretary assumed she was an applicant and Jean wanted to avoid any kind of upsetting situation, so she completed it.

Jean is probably a ____________personality.

b. Sally Thomas is an extrovert, eager for excitement and adventure. Sally would like to be a world traveler, going from one new and exciting place to another. Answers on Sally's application blank have been crossed out with big, definite marks and changed often, indicating that she seems to exchange one good idea for another quite readily.

Sally is probably a ____________personality.

c. Marie Nolton is an artist and an extreme individualist. She describes herself as stylish and somewhat temperamental but quite tolerant of other people. However, Marie really upset Mr. Dawson last week during a phone conversation when she became somewhat irritated at the delay in finding a match and told him that the company should replace him with a computer.

Marie is probably a ____________personality.

d. Barry Clark is an up-and-coming executive with an overwhelming desire to be president of his corporation. Barry describes himself as outgoing, energetic, aggressive, and extremely interested in particular sports. Barry also has some very clear ideas about the type of individual he would like to meet.

Barry is probably a ____________personality.

e. Sam Higgins is an innovative and creative school principal. Sam thinks of himself as an intellectual reformer, but admits that he relies on his assistant to take the actions necessary to implement most of his innovative ideas.

Sam is probably a ____________personality.

f. Rich Gordon is a member of the Dew Valley Country Club, Secret Order of Top-Notchers, and a City Council representative. Rich is very concerned about the possibility of his friends finding out that he has applied to XYZ because it might damage his reputation for respectability and stability. However, Rich is so busy with meetings that he can't find time to meet a single girl on his own.

Rich is probably a ____________personality.

Now, on the basis of color compatibility, match the six people into the best combinations.

g. Sally ____________
h. Jean ____________
i. Marie ____________

j. Jerry, the manager of XYZ, loves his job because it lets him see the excitement in other people's lives while remaining quite detached and uninvolved.

Jerry is probably a ____________personality.

k. Jerry would never date ____________or ____________.
l. But he would consider dating____________if the match he proposes doesn't work out.

Section Three: Applied Color

This section of the color quotient test is based upon color indicators of personality and compatibility combined with information on applied color. Although in a real-life situation, factors other than color, such as form, would need to be considered, this section is to be completed on the basis of the best selection in terms of color only.

1. Amy Reed's four-year-old son, Ronnie, is an extremely bright, energetic child who at times appears to be in perpetual motion. It is often difficult to get Ronnie to sleep at night, and often he is awakened by a particularly bad dream. If you were Amy, what colors would you choose from the following possibilities to decorate Ronnie's room?

a. red/green
b. yellow/red
c. yellow/blue
d. blue/green

2. The Magic Wand Beauty Salon promotes an image of style, glamour, and sophistication. Of the following color combinations, which would be most likely to promote that impression?

a. red, pink, white
b. green, yellow, white
c. purple, lavender, white
d. blue, green, white

3. The New You Beauty Salon is known for its dedication to clean active health. Which of the following color combinations would be the best for the interior color scheme of the New You?

a. red, pink, white
b. green, yellow, white
c. purple, lavender, white
d. blue, green, white

4. You are the advertising manager of an old and established company whose line of furniture is well known to the public. From the four possibilities listed, decide on the best use of your $10,000 magazine advertising budget for this month. Your goals are to keep the company's name before the public in both old and new markets.

a. Ten black-and-white, half-page advertisements in five magazines which have a mixed subscriber list of all ages and all socio-economic backgrounds.

b. Two four-color, full-page ads in two different magazines. One has a readership of individuals between the ages of 25 and 40; the other has a readership of financially established readers of all ages.

c. One four-color, two-page spread in the most expensive and sophisticated trade journal of its kind.

d. One four-color, full-page advertisement in an established trade journal and two black-and-white, full-page ads in two different magazines; one is a new publication which appeals to the reader of 22 to 35 years of age; the other is an established magazine with a subscriber list of retired and semi-retired persons.

5. You are the director of an international social center. Many of the members who are new to this country do not know English. In order to effectively communicate the information in Column A, select the most appropriate color from Column B and write the letter in the space.

Column A		Column B
Electrical Wires—Danger	______	a. white
Step Down—Hazard	______	b. green
Restaurant	______	c. red
First-Aid Supplies	______	d. orange
Health and Exercise Room	______	e. yellow

6. Lynn Gilbert has been depressed and finds it difficult to get excited about anything in life. Lynn would benefit most from an environment which was made up of which set of colors?

a. blue, green, violet
b. red, orange, yellow

7. Marty Peters is a likable, highly qualified employee. However, Marty has been so tense, anxious, and fearful of making mistakes during the past few weeks that the office manager has to decide on a course of action to remedy the situation. The office manager is basically a yellow personality. Would the manager:

a. fire Marty?
b. ignore the situation?
c. redecorate Marty's office in blues and greens?
d. give Marty a red typewriter?

The following situations are all related to each other.

8. Lee Howard has just opened a new real estate office. Lee is a financially successful real estate broker whose hard work, aggressiveness, energy and logic have led to both success and an esteemed reputation. Lee's personality is probably a:

a. green-blue
b. red-yellow
c. red-green
d. yellow-brown personality.

9. Lee has just interviewed four candidates for two secretarial openings in his new office. *Secretary One* will handle all correspondence, act as a receptionist, answer the telephone, and be responsible for maintaining a current and eye-catching wall display of available properties. *Secretary Two* will be responsible for typing new listings, keeping listing books current and organized, maintaining daily books and records, and filing.

Each candidate has the necessary skills and qualifications to handle the secretarial work. However, by asking for opinions on the color scheme for the new office, Lee has found out that each candidate has a definite first and second color preference. On the basis of color preference, compatibility, and job function, select the best candidate for each position.

a. Jamie Ryan: yellow/purple ____________________
b. Chris Sage: purple/red ____________________
c. Alex Avery: green/blue ____________________
d. Kyle Johns: gray/black ____________________

10. Lee is also hiring a sales representative to add to the sales force, which will be transferred from other offices. The sales representative must be outgoing, open and creative, and personally well organized. In addition, the sales representative must work with two other individuals who are a red/green and a yellow/purple personality, respectively. As with the secretarial candidates, Lee has also discovered the color preferences of those applying for the sales position.

a. Del Martin: green/brown
b. Darby Hewitt: red/yellow
c. Fran Thomas: yellow/green
d. Robin Gates: purple/blue

Which candidate will make the best selection? ____________________

11. Lee wants the receptionist's area, which is also the waiting room for prospective clients, to have a serene, comfortable, cheerful atmosphere. Which of the following combinations would be best for this purpose?

a. yellow, green, black
b. orange, yellow, brown
c. blue, green, yellow
d. red, orange, blue

12. The sales representatives' office has a folding door and is opened up for staff meetings that relate to new ideas for promotion, advertising, sales approaches, and client conferences relating to property purchases. This room should have more (warm; cool—select one) colors in order to enhance this purpose and to promote a feeling of action and decision on the part of prospective clients.

13. The office of *Secretary Two*, who performs routine, organizational, and clerical tasks, is also used as a conference room to discuss problems related to employee benefits, listing procedures, and so on. Based on this, plus the functions performed by *Secretary Two*, this room would be most effectively decorated with an emphasis on the (warm; cool—select one) colors.

14. Lee is choosing a carpet for the office. Because it is economically sound and because Lee wants to develop a basic decorating scheme that makes the offices appear to belong to a stable, solid unit, one color will be used throughout the office. Which of the following will provide the best choice and be most adaptive to coordination with the accents necessary for the functions performed in the separate offices?

a. orange/yellow tweed
b. dark red
c. green/blue tweed
d. brown

15. Three sales prospects have been interviewed and the sales representative found out their color choices by again asking opinions on interior color schemes. Three properties in the right price range are available as follows:

a. An old Victorian home on a comfortable, quiet city street
b. A modern split-level in a new and open suburb
c. A remodeled farmhouse on twenty-five acres of land in a country setting.

The clients are:

(1) Donna (blue) and Carl (green) Fillmore ________
(2) Kim Markey(yellow) ________
(3) Rene Taber (brown) ________

Match each property to the best prospect.

Answers to Color Quotient Test

Section One: Personality

A. Red, d; blue, f; brown, c; yellow, e; purple, g; black, h; gray, b; green, a *(8 points)* ______

B. 1. Green *(1 point)* ______

2. a. yellow; b. red; c. brown; d. gray *(4 points)* ______

3. a. blue; b. purple; c. black; d. green-brown; e. black-yellow *(7 points)* ______

C. 1. a. yellow-green; b. red-black; c. blue-purple; d. gray-brown *(8 points)* ______

Section Two: Compatibility

1. Group A: a. Tom; b. Ann; c. Doug—in any order
Group B: d. Pam; e. John; f. Sue—in any order *(6 points)* ______

g. Probably Group B, because the personalities are generally more quiet, stable, nonaggressive (or similar answer) *(2 points)* ______

h. Doug *(1 point)* ______

2.

a.	blue	g.	Barry
b.	red	h.	Rich
c.	purple	i.	Sam
d.	red	j.	gray
e.	yellow	k.	Marie or Sally (either order)
f.	green	l.	Jean

(13 points) ______

Possible subtotal = 50
Your subtotal = ______

Section Three: Applied Color

1. d. blue/green *(1 point)* ______

2. c. purple, lavender, white *(1 point)* ______

3. b. green, yellow, white *(1 point)* ______

4. b. −4 points; d. −2 points ______

5.	c., e., d., a., b. *(1 point for each correct answer)*		______
6.	b.	*(1 point)*	______
7.	c. The manager is creative and optimistic and would probably opt for an approach which did not require a drastic decision.	*(1 point)*	______
8.	c.	*(1 point)*	______
9.	a.—Secretary One	*(1 point)*	______
	c.—Secretary Two	*(1 point)*	______
10.	b.	*(1 point)*	______
11.	c.	*(1 point)*	______
12.	warm	*(1 point)*	______
13.	cool	*(1 point)*	______
14.	c.	*(1 point)*	______
15.	(1)—a; (2)—b; (3)—c *(1 point for each correct answer)*		______

Possible subtotal	=	25
Your subtotal	=	______
Highest total	=	75
Your total	=	______

Your Color Quotient

[66–75]—Phenomenal color power
[56–65]—Superior color power
[46–55]—Your color power is above average.
[36–45]—Your color power is average; if you have an interest in color, further study will add to your color power.
[26–35]—You are probably more sensitive to form and shape than to color.
[25 and under]—Try it again!

Bibliography

Birren, Faber. *Color Psychology and Color Therapy.* Secaucus, N.J.: Citadel Press, 1950, 1961; 1979 printing.

Luscher, Dr. Max. *The 4-Color Person.* Joachim Neugroschel, translator. New York, N.Y.: Simon and Schuster, 1979.

____________. *The Luscher Color Test.* Ian A. Scott, translator and editor. New York, N.Y.: Pocket Books, 1971.

Sharpe, Deborah T. *The Psychology of Color and Design.* Chicago, Ill.: Nelson-Hall, 1974.

TEST YOURSELF!

Discover more about yourself, your friends, your family... with this outstanding new series of fascinating and fun test books!

ANALYZE YOUR PERSONALITY THROUGH COLOR

Psychologists have discovered that our emotional and even physical well being is strongly affected by the colors around us. The color red, for example, can suggest a challenge or threat, yellow can cheer people up, green can produce a calming effect.

This innovative book reveals how personalities can also be analyzed in terms of their reactions to color and color preferences. It is possible to influence people, calm a hyperactive child, and even improve a relationship with the right colors.

TEST YOUR COMPATIBILITY

Everyone must develop the ability to relate effectively with one another, whether in a parent-child relationship, husband-wife relationship, or business relationship.

Through this self-scoring test, everyone can analyze their ability to relate to different personality types, and even alter their behavior to increase compatibility.

TEST YOUR I.Q.

Do you know your I.Q.? Most people are curious about their I.Q., but do not know where and how to have themselves tested and the answers analyzed.

Now at long last, here is an actual I.Q. test that can be taken privately or administered to others. This is an authentic test that correlates to the Wechsler and Stanford-Binet tests. Answers and analysis provide on-the-spot fun and insight!

TEST YOUR E.S.P.

We have all experienced eerie senses of anticipating an event before it has happened-seeing an object before it is in front of us, or knowing the face of a person we have never met.

Now, here is a book that examines extrasensory perception and offers ways to develop and practice these powers in everyday life. Numerous tests and games using simple objects such as cards and dice allow everyone to test their powers of telepathy, clairvoyance, precognition, and other psychic phenomena.

$3.95 each